GUINNESS W★RLD RECORDS

GUINNESS WORLD RECORDS™

FEARLESS FEATS

Incredible Records of Human Achievement

D0095831

Collect and
Compare with

WILD LIVES

Outrageous Animal & Nature Records

GUINNESS WORLD RECORDS

FEARLESS FEATS

Incredible Records of Human Achievement

Compiled by Laurie Calkhoven and Ryan Herndon

For Guinness World Records:
Laura Barrett, Craig Glenday, Hein Le Roux, Ben Way

SCHOLASTIC INC.

New York   Toronto   London   Auckland   Sydney
Mexico City   New Delhi   Hong Kong   Buenos Aires

Guinness World Records Limited has a very thorough accreditation system for records verification. However, whilst every effort is made to ensure accuracy, Guinness World Records Limited cannot be held responsible for any errors contained in this work. Feedback from our readers on any point of accuracy is always welcomed.

ISBN 0-439-71565-2

Cover design by Louise Bova
Interior design by Two Red Shoes Design Inc.
Photo Research by Els Rijper
Records from the Archives of Guinness World Records

12 11 10 9 8 7 6 5 4 3   5/0 6/0 7/0 8/0 9/0

Printed in the U.S.A.

First printing, January 2005

Visit Scholastic.com for information about our books and authors online!

Contents

A Record-Breaking History

The idea for Guinness World Records grew out of a question. In 1951, Sir Hugh Beaver, the managing director of the Guinness Brewery, wanted to know which was the fastest game bird in Europe — the golden plover or the grouse (pictured)? Some people argued that it was the grouse. Others claimed it was the plover. A book to settle the debate did not exist until Sir Hugh discovered the knowledgeable twin brothers Norris and Ross McWhirter.

Like their father and grandfather, the McWhirter twins loved information. They were kids just like you when they started clipping interesting facts from newspapers and memorizing important dates in world history. As well as learning the names of every river, mountain range, and nation's capital, they knew the record for pole squatting (196 days in 1954), which language had only one irregular verb (Turkish), and that the grouse — flying at a timed speed of 43.5 miles per hour — is faster than the golden plover at 40.4 miles per hour.

Norris and Ross served in the Royal Navy during World War II, graduated from college, and launched their own fact-finding business called McWhirter Twins, Ltd. They were the perfect people to compile this book of records that Sir Hugh searched for yet could not find.

The first edition of *The Guinness Book of Records* was published on August 27, 1955. Since then, it has been published in 37 languages and more than 100 countries. In 2000, the book title changed to *Guinness World Records*. It has set an incredible record of its own: Excluding non-copyrighted books such as the Bible and the Koran, *Guinness World Records* is the bestselling book of all time!

Today, the official Keeper of the Records keeps a careful eye on each Guinness World Record, compiling and verifying the greatest the world has to offer — from the fastest and the tallest to the heaviest and the smallest, with everything in between.

They Did What?

For 50 years, Guinness World Records has been collecting cool facts about the world's most amazing record-breakers. From the youngest to the oldest, the most courageous to the most outrageous, alone and in teams — real people continue to astound us with their strength, skills, and bravery in pursuit of setting a world record.

Out of the thousands of incredible records reviewed by Guinness World Records every year, we selected some fearless feats to share with you. Sail solo across the Atlantic, climb the world's tallest peak, or cross Niagara Falls on a tightrope — these people and their stunning achievements will astonish and inspire you.

Now when the question "They did *what?*" is asked, this book has the answer: "Yes, someone actually did *that!*"

Chapter 1
SKY HIGH

People do all kinds of death-defying deeds to break world records. Some leap out of planes and free-fall faster than the speed limit. Others train from childhood to dive off high cliffs into the shallow waters below. Then there are individuals who blast out of a cannon to sail through the air. Discover the people who make records by jumping into, and falling out of, the sky above us.

Largest FAI-Approved Parachuting Free-Fall Formation

People in Takhli, Thailand, on February 6, 2004, witnessed a new world record when they looked up: the skies filled with skydivers falling in a tight, coordinated pattern (pictured). World Team '04 gathered 357 skydivers from more than 40 countries to create the largest free-fall formation. Careful planning and rehearsals were required to get that many people falling through the air together, not to mention in order and safely. The event was part of the Thailand Royal Sky Celebration, held in honor of the Thai Royal Family. The Royal Thai Air Force supported the parachutists' extraordinary efforts.

Pioneering flights like that of the Wright brothers on December 17, 1903 marked the beginning of the modern aviation era. In 1905, a small group of people recognized the need for an international federation to oversee and certify those incredible aviation feats.

Today the Fédération Aéronautique Internationale (FAI) has more than 100 member-nations, including the National Aeronautic Association (NAA) in the United States. In addition to airplane records, the FAI monitors claims for airships, model aircrafts, spacecrafts, hang gliders, and many human-powered aircraft records.

Farthest Human Cannonball Flight

Some people jump from planes while others climb into a cannon. The world-record distance for a person fired from a cannon is held by David "Cannonball" Smith Sr. On May 29, 1998, "Cannonball" fired himself 185 feet, 10 inches — longer than two tennis courts! During his cannon-propelled flight at Kennywood Park, Pennsylvania, Cannonball soared at an estimated 70 miles per hour. But what goes up must come down. How did he land? In a net! The same kind of safety net used by circus performers was carefully positioned based on the knowledge of how far he would fly, and it caught him at the end of his trip. Cannonball has eight children, five of whom have already become human cannonballs. His son, Dave "The Bullet" Smith Jr. (pictured), shows how flying through the air runs in the family!

Highest Regularly Performed Headfirst Dives

The professional high divers from La Quebrada, Acapulco, in Mexico, aim for the water far, far, far below them! The divers (pictured) range in age from 12 to 50 years old and have been regularly taking the plunge for generations. Their headfirst cliff dives start from a height of 115 feet — about as tall as the top floor of a 10-story building — and end in a pool of water only 12 feet deep! The divers have the added challenge of clearing the cliff's edge by 27 feet in order to avoid the rocks at its base. They must watch the waves and time their plunge when there is enough water to dive into. One mistake can be deadly, but the diving brotherhood has been performing its legendary leaps since 1934.

Longest Banzai Skydive

Skydivers usually leap from airplanes with their parachutes firmly strapped onto their backs. Then there are the "Banzai Skydivers." Japan's Yasuhiro Kubo has been skydiving for over 15 years. He leapt from an airplane cruising at 9,842 feet above Davis, California — *without a parachute*. Incredibly, the diving *doyen* (expert in the field) drifted safely to earth on September 2, 2000. A parachute pack was hurled from the plane just before his legendary leap. A small chute attached to the pack slowed its descent. Yasuhiro caught the plummeting parachute within 50 seconds by using self-steering techniques — a record time for the Banzai Skydive.

Fastest Speed Skydiving – Men and Women

Speeding Through the Clouds

Then there are those who like to go faster than birds can fly. The fastest speed ever reached in a men's speed skydiving competition is an incredible 325.67 miles per hour by Frenchman Michael Brooke during the Millennium Speed Skydiving competition over Gap, France, on September 19, 1999. In Bottens, Switzerland, Italian Lucia Bottari set the women's record by reaching a speed of 268.5 miles per hour. Don't blink or you'll miss them!

How do speed skydivers "step on the gas"? They jump from planes at 13,000 feet in an almost vertical headfirst position. This position decreases wind resistance and increases their speed. Electronic altimeters attached to the skydivers calculate their average speed as they cross the "measuring zone" — between 8,850 to 5,570 feet. So how does a skydiver "put on the brakes"? The jumper changes position to slow down to around 120 miles per hour, allowing the parachute to open safely above 2,260 feet. Talk about breaking the speed limit!

Chapter 2
MAN VS. NATURE

Whether scaling the tallest mountains, diving to the deepest depths, or rowing across the ocean, men and women challenge nature and come out on top!

Mount Everest — Oldest Men and Women Climbers

Mount Everest, in the eastern Himalayas on the Tibet-Nepal border, is the highest mountain peak on Earth at 29,028 feet. In fact, the mountain is rising a few millimeters each year due to geological forces. During a heat wave, the temperature might climb all the way to two degrees . . . below zero! These factors have not stopped people from trying to get to the top, starting with the first successful ascent by Sir Edmund Hillary of New Zealand and Sherpa Tenzing Norgay of Nepal on May 29, 1953. Since then, the mountain has seen many more climbers attempt to set many more records.

SMILES IN KATHMANDU

You're never too young or too old to complete your dreams. Just ask these two!

Yuichiro Miura (pictured top), a 70-year-old Japanese climber, couldn't stop smiling after he returned to Kathmandu. On May 26. 2003, Miura became the oldest male climber to conquer Mount Everest. He had broken the record set two years ago by 65-year-old Tomiyasu Ishikawa (pictured bottom), another Japanese climber. Miura is a famous adventurer in Japan who has also skied down the Himalayas.

Tamae Watanabe, also of Japan, stopped to smile for the camera set up in the base camp at the foot of the mountain in Nepal. The 63-year-old climber successfully completed her attempt to reach the summit. She became the oldest woman to climb Mount Everest on May 16, 2002.

Fastest Seven-Summit Ascent

One mountain and one view just wasn't enough for the United Kingdom's Andrew Salter. He climbed the highest peak on each continent in a record 288 days between May 16, 2000, when he reached the summit of Mount Everest in Nepal (Asia), and February 27, 2001, when he scaled Aconcagua in Argentina (South America). In between, he stood atop Vinson Massif in Antarctica, Mount McKinley in Alaska (North America), Mount Kilimanjaro in Tanzania (Africa), Puncak Jaya in Indonesia (Australasia), and Elbrus in Russia (Europe)! For more Mount Everest, check out the color insert.

Fastest Solo Row Across the Atlantic Ocean

Whether climbing rock or crossing water, people always look for the quickest route. Russia's Fyodor Konyukhov made the fastest solo transatlantic row in 46 days and 4 hours. Starting October 16 through December 1, 2002, he rowed from San Sebastian, Gomera, Canary Islands, Spain, to Port St. Charles, Barbados. His boat was special, too. The *Uralaz*, a 22-foot, 7.2-inch fiberglass boat, had solar panels, a gas cooker, and navigation equipment, but weighed only 1,433 pounds fully loaded.

Deepest Seawater Scuba Dive

Take a deep breath before we dive beneath the waves. The deepest scuba dive was 1,010 feet! John Bennett of the United Kingdom dove off Escarcia Point, Puerto Galera, in the Philippines, on November 6, 2001. Aided by a weighted sled, his descent took over 12 minutes. At the bottom, the high pressure exerted upon his body caused vision loss and muscle spasms. His ascent was much slower to avoid decompression sickness, lasting 9 hours and 36 minutes and using 60 oxygen tanks. Happily, John made a full recovery.

The Bends

Scuba divers face many visible, and invisible, dangers when diving. Sharks are not the only things that scare divers — decompression sickness ("the bends") can also be a killer. The human body absorbs nitrogen gas from breathing compressed air. Nitrogen forms tiny bubbles in the diver's tissues and bloodstream. The deeper the dive, the denser the air and the more nitrogen absorbed. If a diver rises too quickly to the surface, these bubbles are trapped inside the body and cause extreme pain in joints and organs. Severe cases of decompression sickness can lead to death. Rising slowly back to the surface allows the nitrogen to enter the bloodstream, be taken into the lungs, then exhaled. All divers, especially those who dive at extreme depths, take extra care in making slow ascents.

Chapter 3
ON THE ROPES

People get themselves roped into all sorts of record-breaking attempts. Some take their thrill-seeking right to the edge . . . but others cross right over. Some do it upside down, some go up and down, while others tie a blindfold over their eyes so they don't look down. Check out the daring ways people got to the other side.

Longest Tyrolean Traverse

How on earth do you cross one side of a high gorge or canyon — such as the Grand Canyon (pictured) — without going the long way around (or firing yourself from a cannon!)? Here's one answer: it's called a "Tyrolean traverse." It's basically a single rope spanning across the gap. All you need to do is climb onto it and pull yourself across. The longest Tyrolean traverse in the world is across the Elbe River in the Czech Republic, and it was made by Zdenek Kadlec of the Czech Republic's Speleological Society (people who study caves). He uses the traverse as a superfast route to move injured people across the canyon. And he made the 3,128.3-feet crossing in 59 minutes and 6 seconds, smashing the previous record by 347 feet. Be sure to catch the color photo of the amazing Tyrolean traverse in the center of the book.

Largest Mass Bungee Jump

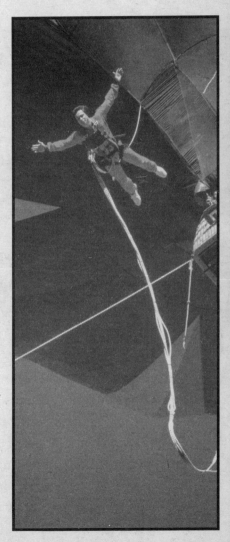

There's jumping for joy and then there's jumping together for the fun of it. A total of 31 people made a bungee jump on the same bungee rope at the Tummelum Record Festival in Flensburg, Germany, on July 8, 2000. The complicated jump began from a gondola suspended at 213 feet from the ground. The event, organized by the Frankfurt City Council, was part of a "skyscraper festival" held to draw public attention to the city's modern architecture.

Bungee cords are made from hundreds of strands of natural rubber bound together with the same material. This man (pictured) counts on the strength and durability of his bungee cord during his leap from a hot-air balloon!

Highest Eight-Person Tightrope Pyramid

Some tightrope walkers turn a stroll into a family day out. The famous American circus troupe The Flying Wallendas performed an eight-person pyramid suspended at a height of 25 feet at Sarasota, Florida, on February 20, 2001. The fearless family performs many such high-wire displays of daring skill and impeccable balance. Here's the Flying Wallendas doing a seven-person pyramid. Can you believe they broke the record by adding one more person?

Longest Time Spent on Tightrope

Tired of keeping your feet on the ground? You could try high-wire walking, such as Adili (pictured) does in China. Or you could move your home like American Jorge Ojeda-Gusman did. He set the tightrope endurance record of 205 days on July 25, 1993. Jorge lived atop a 36-foot-long rope, suspended 35 feet above the ground and attached to two poles. He had a chair on one end and a small wooden cabin (measuring 3 feet x 3 feet) on the other. Jorge ate, slept, washed, and did everything you do . . . just on a tightrope.

First Niagara Falls Tightrope Walk

The great 19-century French tightrope walker, Jean Francois Gravelet, alias Charles Blondin (pictured), defied the dangers of the rapids and the crashing waters below him to complete the first tightrope crossing above Niagara Falls. Thousands arrived on June 28, 1859, to watch his historic walk, but heavy rains prevented Blondin from making his daring attempt. Finally, on June 30, 1859, holding a 40-foot balancing pole, he set out for Canada from the U.S. side of the Falls. The hemp rope was 3 inches thick, 1,100 feet long, and 160 feet above the rushing waters. As he neared the Canadian shore, Blondin surprised everyone by doing a back somersault. Men screamed and women fainted, but he made it safely to the other side of the Niagara River and into the history books.

The Little Wonder

Huge crowds traveled by stagecoach, steamboat, and train to watch Blondin's daring walks in 1859 and 1860. With every crossing, Blondin grew more daring. "The Little Wonder" became his nickname. He journeyed across the Falls on a bike, blindfolded, on stilts, and in the dark with Roman candles flaring from the tips of his balancing pole. He even carried his manager, Harry Colcord, on his back!

One time, he transported a portable stove in a wheel-barrow, paused to cook an omelet, and then shared his meal with passengers on the *Maid of the Mist* steamer floating below!

Today, a statue of Blondin overlooks Niagara Falls, with his wheelbarrow and bicycle on display nearby.

Chapter 4
WHAT A TRIP!

Do you have what it takes to go the distance? Whether cycling 15,000 miles, walking on your hands, or sailing solo across the ocean, these fearless competitors have arrived at the same spot. They've crossed the finish line to make it into the record books.

Youngest Person to Cycle the Pan-American Highway

How about a quick bicycle ride? Try 261 days and 15,234 miles. That's how long it took American Emmanuel Gentinetta (pictured) to finish his solo trip across the Pan-American Highway. He left Prudhoe Bay in Alaska on June 23, 1999, and cycled into Bahia Lapataia in Argentina on March 9, 2000. And he did it aged just 18 years old!

Longest Distance Walking on Hands

Some people like feeling the road beneath their ... palms. In 1900, Johann Hurlinger walked on his hands for 870 miles. In 55 daily 10-hour stints, he journeyed from Vienna to Paris, averaging 1.58 miles per hour.

Johann's record has not been broken in 105 years! Care to try? Better have strong arms, tough hands, and a good sense of balance. This boy is already practicing for his journey. Check out how to be a record-breaker in the back of this book.

Longest Solar-Powered Journey

The driver had to lie down to drive it, but the Radiance solar car won the world record for the longest solar-powered journey. From July 1 to July 29, 2000, it traveled 4,376.62 miles across Canada from Halifax to Vancouver on fuel that cost less than four dollars! Built by the Queens University solar-vehicle team of Ontario, Canada, the Radiance is less than 3.2 feet high and runs on about as much energy as a toaster. It was not only able to convert the sun's rays to energy, it also stored the sun's power by using it to charge more than 1,000 nickel batteries. The support truck that followed behind throughout the duration of the record attempt consumed more than $2,000 of gasoline!

Five Scorching Sun Facts

1. At around 4.6 billion years old, the sun is estimated to be about halfway through its life.

2. It takes light 8.3 minutes to reach us from the sun — at the speed of light, of course!

3. The temperature at the sun's surface is around 9,900°F, and at its core, temperatures reach around 27,000,000°F.

4. A large solar flare can release as much energy as 10,000 million one-megaton nuclear bombs.

5. The sun is so large that it could contain 1.3 million Earths.

Youngest Solo Transatlantic Sailor

Sebastian Clover (pictured) sailed across the Atlantic Ocean single-handedly at the age of 15 years and 362 days. He launched his 2,700-mile journey from Santa Cruz de Tenerife, Canary Islands, Spain, on December 19, 2002, and encountered fierce Atlantic storms and killer whales as big as his yacht. On January 12, 2003, he safely reached English Harbour, Antigua and Barbuda, on the other side of the ocean.

A Close Race

Sebastian set the record while racing his father, Ian, across the Atlantic! Sebastian lost the race — his father is a professional sailing and ocean navigation instructor, after all — but he did win a place in the record books.

Sebastian had trained for his solo crossing for more than three years before he raced against his father. The two kept in contact via cell phone for almost the entire trip — except for one morning when Sebastian's cell-phone battery ran out. The previous day, a pod of killer whales had closely tailed Sebastian's boat before finally moving on. Maybe they were in on the race, too!

Most Tour de France Wins

American Lance Armstrong was practically born on a bike! After competing in triathlons (races where contestants run, swim, and cycle), he focused on cycling at age 16. He turned professional after the 1992 Olympic Games, yet finished last out of 111 riders in his very first pro race! He went on to win 10 titles the following year. By 1996, he had hit the number one spot when a cancer diagnosis threatened his career. Although only given a 50 percent chance of survival, Lance battled cancer with the same fearless determination he used to win races. In 1998, he was cancer-free and back to racing. In 1999, he won the Tour de France, with the fastest average speed ever. He went on to win the race from 2000 to 2004 becoming the only cyclist in history to win the Tour de France six times! To see Lance in action, take a look at the color insert!

Take a Spin Around France

The Tour de France is the world's most grueling and popular bicycle race. Each July, more than 150 competitors race along a 2,000-mile course of European roads. The course changes every year. It lies mostly in France, but also passes through Belgium, Spain, Germany, and Switzerland. The final stretch always runs along the famous Parisian avenue the Champs-Élysées.

The course is divided into sections, or stages. Some stages emphasize a particular cycling skill such as mountain climbing or sprinting. Cyclists are timed during each stage. One stage in the French Alps included 21 hairpin turns! During the race, the cyclist with the fastest time wears the famous yellow jersey. At the end, the winner receives the yellow jersey at a big celebration in Paris.

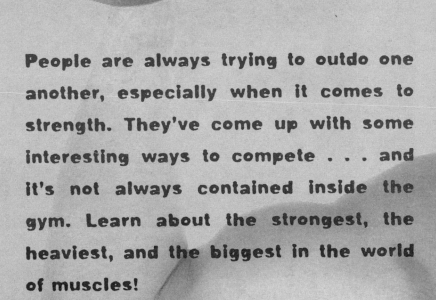

Chapter 5
HEAVE HO!

People are always trying to outdo one another, especially when it comes to strength. They've come up with some interesting ways to compete . . . and it's not always contained inside the gym. Learn about the strongest, the heaviest, and the biggest in the world of muscles!

Heaviest Weight Lifted by Human Beard

Tug on Lithuanian Antanas Kontrimas' beard and he'll pull you right off your feet! Just ask 135-pound Ruta Cekyte. She swung off the ground for 15 seconds holding on to Kontrimas' beard (pictured). This hair-raising event occurred on August 18, 2001, at the VIII International Country Festival 2001 in Visaginas, Lithuania.

Muscle Power

Muscles are the power tools of our bodies. Just as a car engine converts fuel into energy, muscles convert proteins into chemical energy for our bodies. Skeletal muscles working in pairs move our bones. Our brain tells muscles which way to move. When people "flex their muscles," millions of tiny protein filaments convert chemicals into energy, and the muscles respond by tensing and contracting, helping you lift or pull heavy objects. The *masseter* is the strongest muscle in the human body. Do you know where it is? The masseter is the jaw muscle that helps you eat, talk, and, with some people, pull trains!

Fastest Boeing 737 Pull By a Team

It was a team effort. Ten Royal Marine reserves (pictured) got together to flex their muscles at Manchester Airport, United Kingdom. The team pulled a Boeing 737-300 airplane, weighing 81,500 pounds, over a distance of 328 feet. They achieved this feat on January 27, 2001, in an astonishing 43.2 seconds!

Skull Strength Record-Breaker

John Evans holds many records for his feats of amazing strength, including Balancing the Most Milk Crates on the Head (96!) and Balancing the Heaviest Car on the Head – although not at the same time! On May 24, 1999, John balanced a gutted Mini car, weighing 352 pounds, on his head for 33 seconds at the London Studios, London, United Kingdom. Over the years, John has set more than 20 records in 11 categories, but the head-strong heavyweight continues to look for new Guinness World Records to attempt. John's amazing skills are on display in full color in the center of the book!

Heaviest Vehicle Pulled with Teeth

Good tooth care is important for Walter Arfeuille of Belgium. He has lifted weights totaling 620 pounds 10 ounces using only his teeth! Walter also used his strong bite to pull a train. Eight railway carriages weighed 493,570 pounds, but Walter pulled the train along the rails for a distance of 10 feet 5 inches. The amazing human train pull (pictured) took place on June 9, 1996, in Diksmuide, Belgium. See, we told you that the jaw muscle was the strongest in the body! Believe us now?

Largest Yokozuna Sumo Wrestler

Supersized Wrestling

Hawaiian-born Chad Rowan, alias Akebono (pictured), became the first foreign *rikishi* (wrestler) to be promoted to the top rank of *yokozuna* (grand champion) in January 1993. He is the tallest yokozuna in sumo history at 6 feet 8 inches high. He is also the heaviest, weighing 501 pounds. How would you like to face him in the wrestling ring?

Sumo wrestling is an ancient Japanese sport that began as a performance in the Shinto religion. Many of the ancient rituals are still practiced today.

Size, strength, and weight are major factors for a sumo's success. These highly trained athletes follow special diets to maintain their weight, which is usually more than 300 pounds.

A contestant loses if he is forced out of the 15-foot circular ring. He also cannot let any part of his body, other than the soles of his feet, touch the ground. Once a wrestler becomes yokozuna, he keeps his title forever. However, if he begins to lose matches, he is expected to retire.

Chapter 6
SENSATIONAL SKILLS

All records require special skills. Some skills required to set certain records are a bit more sensational than others.

House of Cards with Most Stories

Breathless and steady-handed, Bryan Berg built a 127-story tower out of 1,200 packs of playing cards, without using any adhesives such as tape or glue. His freestanding house, built at the College of Design at Iowa State University, was 24 feet 4 inches tall. That was in May 1999. On November 6, 1999, the architecture graduate broke his own record with a 131-story house of cards. This amazing structure used 1,765 packs of cards and weighed 242 pounds 8 ounces! Want to see another one of Bryan's amazing structures? There's a color photo in the insert!

Most Clothespegs Clipped on a Face

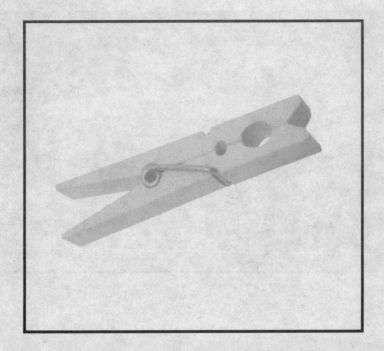

Garry Turner has a rare skin disorder that causes his skin to stretch like rubber. It has also won him world records! His favorite trick is to stretch the skin from his neck over his mouth to create the "human turtleneck." Garry broke his own previous record on July 20, 2004, in the London offices of Guinness World Records, when he clipped 154 wooden clothespegs to his face! There's a color photo of this amazing feat in the center of the book.

Sitting in a Bathtub with the Most Snakes

Jackie Bibby is fearless around snakes. He has worn them on his head, held them in his mouth (see the front cover of this book), and has chilled out with his hissing friends in a bathtub. Jackie and Rosie Reynolds-McCasland of Texas share the record for sitting in a bathtub with the most live rattlesnakes. Jackie and Rosie sat in two separate tubs, each with 75 western diamondback rattlesnakes, on September 24, 1999, in Los Angeles, California.

Most Chainsaw Juggling Throws

Why would someone juggle chainsaws? Ask Tom Comet of Canada, who juggled three gas-driven chainsaws for 44 throws (14 complete rotations and 2 catches) on August 5, 2002, at Princess Street Gardens, Edinburgh, United Kingdom. Comet broke the record of 12 rotations set by Karoly Donnert on *Guinness Rekord TV* in Stockholm, Sweden, on January 30, 2001. Don't try this at home! Tom is a professional chainsaw juggler with years of experience.

Most Prolific Record-Breaker

Ashrita Furman, of New York City, is Guinness World Records' Top Record-Holder. He's set or broken more than 80 records — and although some of his records have since been broken, he still holds 22! He's always coming up with new ideas and new records to break. Here are just a few of the titles he currently holds:

Greatest Distance Jumped on a Pogo Stick: 23.11 miles on June 22, 1997.

Milk Crate Balancing on Chin: Ashrita balanced a total of 23 milk crates on his chin for 11.23 seconds on June 17, 2002.

Longest Milk Bottle Head Balancing Walk: He won this record by walking with a milk bottle balanced on his head without stopping for 80.96 miles.

Most Hopscotch Games in 24 Hours: In January 1998, he completed 434 games of hopscotch in Cancún, Mexico, to win this world record.

Most Skips in 24 Hours: Ashrita traveled all the way to Indonesia to set this record. From January 23–24, 1999, he achieved 130,000 skips on a rope in 24 hours, but someone else has since claimed the record. Time for Ashrita to try again!

Here, Ashrita balances pint glasses on his chin!

Breaking Records My Way

Ashrita Furman holds more world records than any other person. As a teenager, he says he was bad at sports . . . until he discovered the world of record-breaking. "Guinness World Records says to me that you can do anything if you try," he says. "Pick something you might be good at."

Ashrita first made it into the Guinness World Records book in 1979 by doing 27,000 jumping jacks. To date, he has not stopped trying — and succeeding — at setting more records! For more Ashrita, check out the insert!

Chapter 7
ALL A-BOARD

Climb on board and hang on for a wild ride with these competitors! On land or sea, in a roller coaster or on a surfboard attached to a kite, these people enjoy their ride into the record books.

Most Surfing Championships Won

Men: American Kelly Slater has won the men's Surfing World Championships title a record six times, in 1992 and 1994 to 1998. Kelly grew up in Florida idolizing the kings of the waves who surfed in Hawaii and Australia. He was determined to compete and entered his first surfing competition at the age of eight. He started winning in competitions that same year and has continued to carve the waves with his surfboard around the world.

Women: The most ASP (Association of Surfing Professionals) Tour World Championship titles won by a woman is six, by Australian Layne Beachley from 1998 to 2003.

FROM THE TIPS OF THEIR TOES . . .

© Gary Rothwell

BOOTS OF FIRE

Daredevil motorcyclist Gary Rothwell sets off sparks during his world-record road trips. His titanium boots protect more than his feet at speeds of 204.4 miles per hour. His boots skim — not grip — the surface of the road while he holds on to the back of his 1300cc Suzuki Hayabusa, the world's fastest production motorcycle. Catch up to Gary in "Daring Feats of Feet."

TO THE TOPS OF THEIR HEADS

GUINNESS WORLD RECORDS

DUDE, WHERE'S MY CAR?
The secrets of success for a professional "Head Balancer"? A sturdy stance and a strong neck. John Evans must maintain his own balance or the load falling off his head will crush him. The strongest part of his body is his 24-inch neck, not his arms. Read more about John in "Heave Ho!"

GOT MILK?
Multiple record-holder Ashrita Furman stands still, instead of walking and running with a milk bottle balanced on his head — only 2 out of his 40-plus world-record collection. Keep your eyes peeled for more of Ashrita in "Sensational Skills."

THESE INCREDIBLE PEOPLE

Walk Farther

SKYWALKER
Mike Howard walks the plank between two hot-air balloons aloft at 18,800 feet. Safety ropes kept the balloons traveling together while Mike, without a parachute, completed his stroll. Find more fearless walks in "Daring Feats of Feet" and wild journeys in "What a Trip!"

GUINNESS WORLD RECORDS ™

Try Harder

© Peter DeJong/AP/Wide World Photos

LANCE TOURS FRANCE

Although he was last in his very first race, Lance Armstrong kept trying and overcame many challenges — personal and professional — to become the only cyclist in history to win the grueling Tour de France bicycle competition six times. Left, he pedals past the Eiffel Tower. Race over to "What a Trip!" for more details.

© 2001 Drew Gardner / Guinness World Records

WHAT'S ON YOUR FACE?

Having the stretchiest skin allows Garry Turner to withstand the pinch of many wooden clothespins. Garry's rare skin condition is Ehlers-Danlos syndrome (EDS), which allows him to stretch his skin like a rubber band — he can even pull his neck skin over his mouth to create the "human turtleneck"! Learn how people deal with their very different body types in "Life Stories."

LEGGO MY POGO!

There goes Ashrita Furman again — trying for another world record. He recently set a pogo-stick record in Antarctica . . . even when the spring of the pogo froze and fell off! "Keep trying" is Ashrita's motto.

STEADY AS HE BUILDS

Bryan Berg has patience, an eye for detail, determination, and steady hands when building his house of cards. As a kid, he developed his sensational skills in building strong card towers to withstand his brother's efforts to blow them down. See how others outlast nature's attempts to knock them down in "Man vs. Nature."

Climb Higher

© Bobby Model/National Geographic Image Collection

TOP OF THE WORLD

Climbers who answer the challenge of the world's highest mountain must survive many dangers, including the Khumbu Icefall. There is no quick, fast, or safe route to reach the top. Ropes, picks, ladders, and good teammates are necessary during the climb. Rappel over to the Mount Everest section in "Man vs. Nature."

Cling Tighter

GET TO THE OTHER SIDE

Why did this man cross over the Elbe River? He was just doing his job! The Czech Speleological Emergency Service ran this static rope — called a "Tyrolean traverse" — over the river in case they needed to rescue people stranded on the other side. Hang out with other record-holders in "On the Ropes."

Soar Faster

© Photo: Flexifoil

GO SURF A KITE

Jason Furness enjoys the latest extreme sport, kite surfing, while crossing the English Channel. The special kite, manufactured by Flexifoil International, attaches to a custom-made wakeboard. The surfer controls the kite to catch air currents and propel his board into the "power zone," where wind pushes his board to its fastest speed. Surf over to "All A-Board" for more amazing records.

. . . TO BE A GUINNESS WORLD RECORD-HOLDER!

Oldest Barefoot Water-Skier

American "Banana George" Blair of Winter Haven, Florida, likes to keep moving all year round. Born on January 22, 1915, George celebrates his birthday by pulling on his bright yellow wet suit, tossing his shoes aside, strapping on a pair of skis, and going for a spin around the lake (pictured). On February 10, 2002, he skied barefoot on Lake Florence, Florida. Being 87 years and 18 days old at the time, he skied into the record books as the world's Oldest Barefoot Water-skier! George also likes hitting the slopes between 45 and 60 days a year and is the Oldest Active Snowboarder in the world!

Largest Motorcycle Pyramid

The Daredevil Team of the Indian Army Signal Corps achieved a motorcycle pyramid consisting of 210 men balanced on only 10 motorcycles on July 5, 2001, at Gowri Shankar Parade Ground, Jabalpur, India. The pyramid traveled a distance of 424 feet.

Forming *castells* or human pyramids is a tradition in the Catalan town of Tarassa, Spain. Spectators gathered to see this ten-story castell (pictured, November 2, 1998). Everybody hold on!

Roller Coaster Marathon

American Richard Rodriguez (pictured front) rode the Expedition GeForce and Superwirbel roller coasters at Holiday Park, Hassloch, Germany, for 192 hours (eight days) nonstop from August 20 to 28, 2003. An earlier attempt at the record, five weeks before, ended when a serious thunderstorm shut down all the rides for 45 minutes. Richard had been riding the coasters at that point for six complete days!

Fastest Crossing of the English Channel by Kite Surfer

Chris Calthrop, Jason Furness, and Andy Preston (all from the U.K.) crossed the English Channel using kite surfers – custom-made boards with 52-foot kites – on September 17, 1999. They began in one country (the United Kingdom) and landed in another (France) at different times. Although they all completed the 23.2-nautical-mile crossing in record-breaking time, two members clocked in at 2 hours 30 minutes while the third surfer ended his ride at three hours.

Kite Surfing – The Newest Extreme Water Sport

Kite surfing (aka kiteboarding and fly-surfing) combines windsurfing, wakeboarding, surfing, paragliding, and power kiting all in one. Invented by the French and made popular in Hawaii, kite surfers are now ripping across waters all over the world.

The idea behind kite surfing is simple. A person stands on a board, similar to a wakeboard or a surfboard but with foot straps or bindings, and uses a kite to capture the power of the wind and propel them across the water. The kite surfer must pilot the kite while steering the board, making this new sport extremely challenging.

Athletes who love ripping across the water and soaring into the air can experience both in the same sport. Some kite surfers are experimenting with blending other board sports. Some are attaching their kites onto snowboards, making this a year-round, all-weather sport!

For a great view of this custom gear in action, flip over to Jason Furness in the color insert!

Chapter 8
LIFE STORIES

Many people deliberately set out to break world records. They train and practice and work hard. Others set records because of who they are and how they live life – courageously!

Tallest Man

The tallest man who ever lived was Robert Pershing Wadlow of the United States, who grew to 8 feet 11.1 inches. At birth in 1918, Robert weighed a regular 8.5 pounds. But by the time he started school at the age of five, he was wearing a suit made for a 17-year-old. When he was eight, his 6-foot 2-inch body was too big for his school desk! Because he was so tall, the "Gentle Giant" had poor circulation in his legs and limited sensation in his feet. He died in his sleep in 1940 after living as normal a life as possible, despite his extraordinary size.

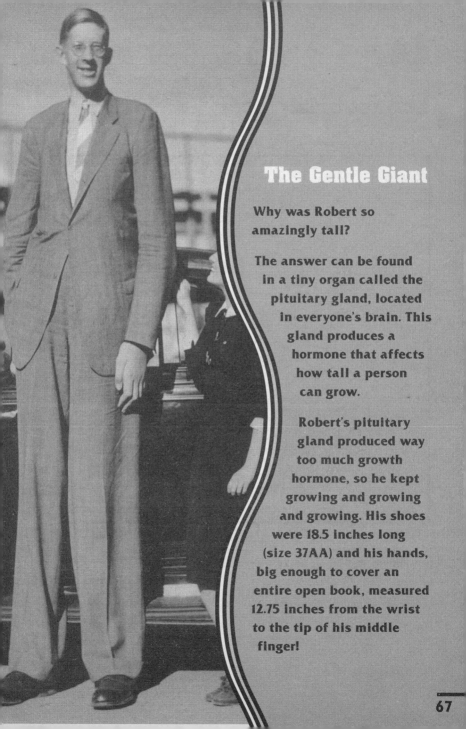

The Gentle Giant

Why was Robert so amazingly tall?

The answer can be found in a tiny organ called the pituitary gland, located in everyone's brain. This gland produces a hormone that affects how tall a person can grow.

Robert's pituitary gland produced way too much growth hormone, so he kept growing and growing and growing. His shoes were 18.5 inches long (size 37AA) and his hands, big enough to cover an entire open book, measured 12.75 inches from the wrist to the tip of his middle finger!

Longest Hair

How would you like to wash and dry almost 17 feet of hair?

The world's longest documented hair belonged to Hoo Sateow of Thailand, a tribal medicine man. He stopped cutting his hair in 1929, believing that it held the key to his healing powers. On November 21, 1997, his unbound hair was officially measured at 16 feet, 11 inches long.

Oldest Person Ever

Jeanne-Louise Calment lived to an astounding 122 years and 164 days old when she died in France on August 4, 1997. Born in France on February 21, 1875, she was 14 when the Eiffel Tower was finished in 1889. She led an active life – fencing at 85 years old and still riding a bicycle at 100! At the age of 114, she became the oldest actress in film when she played herself in the French movie *Vincent and Me*!

Longest Fingernails

American Lee Redmond knows the secret of good nail care: Eat high protein, soak them in warm olive oil, enjoy a nice manicure, and don't chew on them. Since 1979, Lee has grown her nails to an astonishing length of 24 feet 7.8 inches! Lee wanted to see how long she could grow her nails before they twisted . . . except they didn't, so she kept growing them, and growing and growing . . . !

Longest Tongue

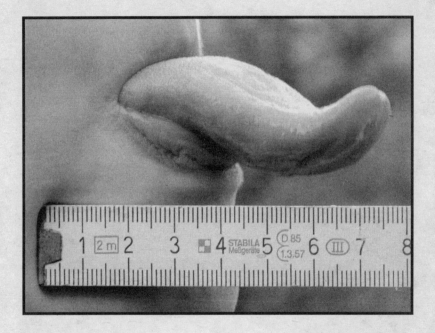

No, the longest tongue doesn't belong to a rock star. Stephen Taylor of the United Kingdom has a very long tongue that measures 3.7 inches from the tip to the center of his closed top lip. It was measured in Warwickshire, United Kingdom, on May 29, 2002.

Ready to measure your tongue? Grab a ruler and say, "Aaahh!"

Chapter 9
FANTASTIC FOOD FEATS

You ate what? From where? These competitors chose to munch their way into the history books. Check out that bowl before you grab a spoon — is it spaghetti or is it . . . worms?!

Most Eaten in 30 Seconds: Worms

C. Manoharan "Snake Manu" of India knew what was in his bowl before he gulped down the contents. *Eeew!* He ate worms — 200 earthworms, each measuring at least 4 inches long, were fully consumed in 30 seconds at Chennai City, Tamil Nadu, India, on November 15, 2003.

Most Hamburgers Crammed into a Person's Mouth

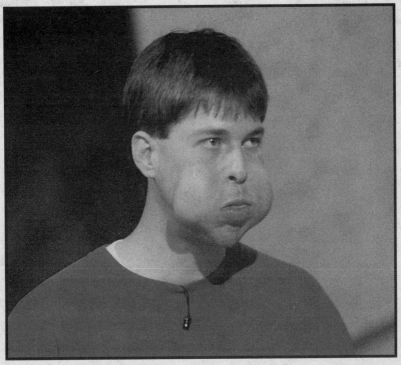

The record for stuffing the most hamburgers (including buns and condiments) in the mouth at one time is three. American Johnny Reitz (pictured) performed this cheek-stretching feat on *Guinness World Records: Primetime* in Los Angeles, California, on June 17, 1998. The rules required he only hold them in his mouth and not swallow any parts of the regulation-size hamburgers.

Bubble Gum Bubble Queen

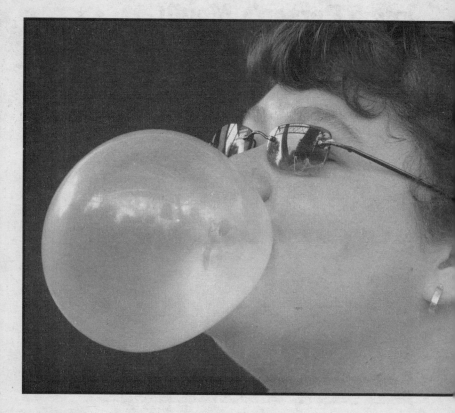

On July 19, 1994, Susan Montgomery Williams (not pictured), armed with three pieces of bubble gum, three previous world records, and 15 years of experience in gum chewing and bubble blowing, blew herself into the record books with a 23-inch pink inflation. That's bigger than a basketball! Susan took her first world record in 1979 and has been popping her own record ever since.

Bigger Bubbles

Although Susan Mont-"gum"-ery has broken her own record three times, she's still waiting for someone to challenge her title as Bubble-Blowing Queen. Sheri McNamara (pictured) won the bubble gum blowing contest at the 2003 Iowa State Fair, but her bubble was only 8 inches big. Why don't you give it a try? Here are some tips from the experts:

1. If you're not having any luck, chew more gum.

2. Don't let the gum warm up too much. Even though warmer gum is easier to blow, colder gum holds the bubble longer!

3. Make sure you chew the gum until it loses its sugary flavor. All brands of gum contain sugar, and sugar doesn't stretch!

4. Blow, blow, blow!

Human Ice Cube

He uses yoga and breathing exercises to help his body prepare for his subzero record attempts. Wearing only his swimming trunks, Wim Hof of the Netherlands (pictured) was able to endure standing in a tube filled with ice cubes for 1 hour, 7 minutes, beating his previous record by 56 seconds at the studios of *Guinness World Records: Die Grössten Weltrekorde* on January 23, 2004. Hof also currently holds the record for Farthest Breath-Held Swim Beneath Ice.

Largest Ice-Cream Sundae

Ever have an ice-cream-sundae competition? Experts around the world compete to sculpt the biggest sundae out of the usual ingredients for an extra-large helping!

An ice-cream sundae weighing 54,914 pounds (24.91 tons!) was made by Palm Dairies in Edmonton, Alberta, Canada, on July 24, 1999.

Want to make your own?

Here's the recipe:

- 20.27 tons of ice cream (any flavor)

- 4.39 tons of syrup

- 537 pounds, 3 ounces of toppings

- and as many spoons as you have friends.

Dig in!

Chapter 10

DARING FEATS OF . . . FEET

These feet are made for walking – and skiing, and balancing, and even for shooting arrows. Some challengers rely on their skillful feet to break records!

Farthest Distance Shot With a Bow and Arrow Using the Feet

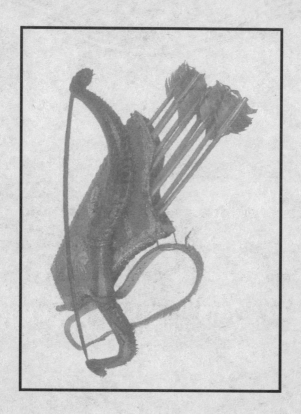

Argentina's Claudia Gomez is a bit of a sharpshooter when it comes to the bow and arrow — or should that be toe and arrow? The nimble-footed archer set a record for firing a bow 18 feet 4 inches . . . using just her feet!

Highest Altitude for a Balloon Skywalk

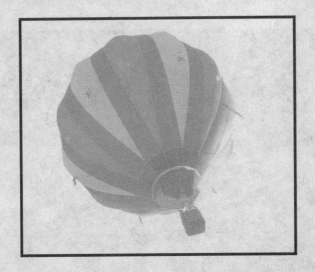

Pirates didn't make him do it, but on May 20, 1998, Mike Howard of the United Kingdom walked the plank – literally. Howard walked, with no parachute, between two hot-air balloons at the frightening height of 18,800 feet – the highest altitude at which anyone has ever completed a balloon skywalk. The balloons, connected by two safety ropes, flew over Marshall, Michigan, with Howard balancing on a tiny plank 19 feet long and only 3 inches wide. By the time he finished his return journey across the beam, the balloons had risen a further 200 feet, taking the daredevil to the dizzy height of 19,000 feet! Want to see this amazing act for yourself? There's a color picture in the middle of the book!

Farthest Distance Walked on Water

In 1988, Remy Bricka (pictured) of France "walked" across the Atlantic Ocean on polyester ski floats 13 feet, 9 inches long. Leaving Tenerife, Canary Islands, Spain, on April 2, 1988, he covered 3,502 miles, arriving in Trinidad on May 31, 1988. Remy made his extraordinary two-month journey eating plankton on the way. His next challenge is to walk across the Pacific Ocean. He has attempted it once, but had to cancel his plans — stay tuned!

Fastest Speed Road Skiing Behind a Motorcycle

Gary Rothwell began riding motorbikes in 1984 at the age of 13. Today he's a professional motorbike stuntman who enjoys riding his motorcycle in his own unique style: by hanging off the seat and land-skiing in his titanium boots . . . at speeds over 156 miles per hour! See the sparks fly — check out Gary Rothwell's daredevil *feet* in the color insert!

Longest Toenails

In 1991, the combined length of Californian Louise Hollis' 10 toenails was 87 inches! Louise has 12 children and 21 grand-children, many of whom lend a hand to help paint and file her unique "col-lection."

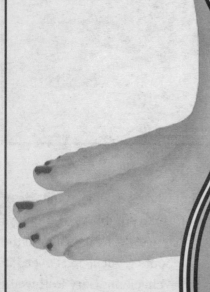

Toe Wrestling

The sport of toe wrestling resembles arm wrestling – but you use your toes. Regulars at Ye Olde Royal Oak Inn in Wetton, England, invented a sport in the hopes of guaranteeing their own victories.

Competitors – without footwear, of course – try to push their opponent's foot to the other side of a ring called a "toe–rack" using only their toes. Wrestlers lock toes and the match begins with the command "Toes away!" Winners must take the best of three "toe-downs." If someone is in pain and wants to give in, he or she can call "toe much" to end the match.

Only people with a toe-riffic sense of humor will win at this sport!

BE A
Record-Breaker!

Message from the Official Keeper of the Records:
Record-breakers are the ultimate in one way or
the other – the youngest, the oldest, the tallest, the
smallest. So how do you get to be a record-breaker?
Follow these important steps:

1. Before you attempt your record, check with us to
make sure your record is suitable and safe. First, get
your parents' permission. Next, contact one of our
officials by using the record application form at
www.guinnessworldrecords.com.

2. Tell us about your idea. Give us as much information as you can, including what the record is, when
you want to attempt it, where you'll be doing it, and
so on.

   a) We will tell you if a record already exists,
   what safety guidelines you must follow during
   your attempt to break that record, and what
   evidence we need as proof that you completed
   your attempt.

   b) If your idea is a brand-new record nobody

has set yet, we need to make sure it meets our requirements. If it does, then we'll write official rules and safety guidelines specific to that record idea and make sure all attempts are made in the same way.

3. Whether it is a new or existing record, we will send you the guidelines for your selected record. Once you receive these, you can make your attempt at any time. You do not need a Guinness World Record official at your attempt. But you do need to gather evidence. Find out more about the kind of evidence we need to see by visiting our website.

4. Think you've already set or broken a record? Put all of your evidence as specified by the guidelines in an envelope and mail it to us at Guinness World Records.

5. Our officials will investigate your claim fully – a process that can take up to 10 weeks, depending on the number of claims we've received and how complex your record is.

6. If you're successful, you will receive an official certificate that says you are now a Guinness World Record-Holder!

Need more info? Check out the Kids' Zone on *www.guinnessworldrecords.com* for lots more hints and tips and some top record ideas that you can try at home or at school. Good luck!

Photo Credits

6 Free-Fall Formation, © Henny Winggers, World Team, HO/ AP Wide World Photos

9 Human Cannonball, © Springfield News Leader, Dean Curtis/ AP Wide World Photos

11 Cliff Divers, © Danny Lehman/CORBIS

16 Oldest Mount Everest Climber — Male, © Gopal Chitrakar/Reuters/CORBIS

16 Oldest Mount Everest Climber — Female, © Office Seven Summits, HO/ AP Wide World Photos

25 Bungee Jumper, © Jamie Budge/CORBIS

26 The Flying Wallendas, © Richard Sheinwald/ AP Wide World Photos

27 High Wire Act, © Xinhua Yang Lei/AP Wide World Photos

28 Charles Blondin, © Hulton-Deutsch Collection/Corbis

32 Epic Pan Am, Mario A. Gentinetta/Courtesy of Guinness World Records

33 El-Molo Boy Doing Handstands, © Jeffrey L. Rotman/CORBIS

34 Radiance Solar Car, © Trevor Collens/ AP Wide World Photos

36 Seb Clover, © Colin James/AP Wide World Photos

42 Beard Lift, Antanas Kontrimas/Courtesy of Guinness World Records